TOP TIPS:
WORSHIPPING WITH
UNDER-5S

Alison Dayer

Copyright © Scripture Union 2011
First published 2011
ISBN 978 1 84427 568 7

Scripture Union England and Wales
207–209 Queensway, Bletchley,
Milton Keynes, MK2 2EB, England
Email:info@scriptureunion.org.uk
Website: www.scriptureunion.org.uk

Scripture Union Australia,
Locked Bag 2, Central Coast Business
Centre, NSW 2252
Website: www.scriptureunion.org.au

Scripture Union USA
PO Box 987, Valley Forge, PA 19482
Website: www.scriptureunion.org

The right of Alison Dayer to be
identified as the author of this work
has been asserted by her in
accordance with the Copyright,
Designs and Patents Act 1988.

British Library Cataloguing-in-
Publication Data: a catalogue record
of this book is available from the
British Library.

Printed and bound in Singapore by
Tien Wah Press Ltd.

Logo, cover design, internal design:
www.splash-design.co.uk
Internal illustrations: Colin Smithson
Typesetting: Richard Jefferson, Author
and Publisher Services

Scripture Union is an
international Christian charity working
with churches in more than 130
countries, providing resources to bring
the good news about Jesus Christ to
children, young people and families
and to encourage them to develop
spiritually through the Bible and
prayer.

As well as our network of volunteers,
staff and associates who run holidays,
church-based events and school
Christian groups, we produce a wide
range of publications and support
those who use our resources through
training programmes.

CONTENTS

INTRODUCTION

It's Wednesday morning and the local church is quiet. Its car park is almost empty. Then vehicles begin to arrive. Small children and adults get out and move quickly towards the front door which stands open. More families walking with buggies arrive and head straight for the church. From inside comes the sound of lively music. The adults greet each other while the children strain to be released from the buggies. Inside the children run to find their friends and the toys, as the adults chat over hot drinks and biscuits. When everyone has arrived and had time to settle, one adult rings a bell with a mellow chime. 'Time for worship!' she calls and the children rush to an area nearby laid out with mats and cushions facing the cross. When the group has gathered, the worship begins…

But what happens next? If these young children are to worship God, then the opportunity provided for them must meet their needs, enabling them to communicate with him, however young they are. They may not be able to speak fluently yet, but their parents understand and love them. So does God and he is not limited to understanding their words. He knows and loves each child even better than their parents do. How happy he must feel when his youngest friends show him how much they love him.

The word 'worship' refers to showing love, admiration and respect. Worshipping God means showing God how wonderful we think he is. Young children show this sort of love and admiration very easily, to people and to God. I love leading young children in worship – it is such an honour. If you are reading this, you probably want to help young children worship God too. My hope is that this book will inspire you and that my experiences will help you to enjoy this honour – enabling young children to worship their heavenly Father.

PART ONE - BIBLE BASE

Worship in the Bible

The Bible is full of worship. Some parts of the Bible describe how God gives instructions as to how people are to worship him (Deuteronomy 31:19–22; Leviticus 23 and many others). Other parts of the Bible describe God's people worshipping him in many different ways. Singing is prominent with many of the psalms being intended for singing, Miriam (Exodus 15:20,21) and Mary (Luke 1:46–55) spontaneously praising with songs and Jesus and his disciples singing a hymn at the end of the last supper (Matthew 26:30). Prayer is an important aspect of worship in the Bible with Moses (Exodus 34:8,9), Samuel (1 Samuel 12:18), Solomon (1 Kings 8:12), Nehemiah (Nehemiah 1:4), Jesus (Matthew 14:23; John 11:41–42 and many others) and Paul (Acts 16:25) praying to God as part of their relationship with him. Indeed, some Bible transaltions sometimes use 'prayer' where others use 'worship'.

Psalm 150 shows a praise that is exuberant and loud with drums, cymbals, trumpets and tambourines. This is not the decorous worship of an elegant organ, but the excitement of a crowd celebrating their God and his creation. Other examples of exuberant, undignified worship include David dancing and leaping with all his might in praise of God (2 Samuel 6:12–22). Clearly worship can be dignified, calm and gentle (as in many of the examples above), but it can equally be undignified, exciting and loud.

Think about...
Make a list of all the ways you can think of that people use to show their appreciation and thanks to each other. Now think about how you can use these ways to worship God.

Young children in the Bible

In biblical times children were not seen as important in society, so the Bible makes only occasional references specifically to young children. However, those references that are there are significant. Psalm 139:13–16 tells how God knows each child as they form in the womb as he creates them. His love for each of us begins as life begins. When God came to Earth he came as a baby, sharing in the experiences of learning and growing as a human child (Luke 2). Clearly this time must have been worthwhile as preparation for Jesus' adult ministry.

God instructs his people to teach their children about him and his ways (Deuteronomy 6:6,7; Proverbs 22:6). They are to talk about God with their children at all times – at home, out and about, in the morning and in the evening. God wants the children to absorb his story as they live and breathe and so grow in their love for and relationship with him as they grow. It is to be assumed that the main responsibility for this lies with the family, but the community of faith has its part to play. It is the community that holds the families and individuals together in corporate worship and teaching.

Jesus himself valued children and surprised his disciples in doing so. When parents brought their children to Jesus for a blessing, his disciples tried to send them away, saying Jesus was too busy. But Jesus was adamant that he had time for the children. He wanted to spend time with them, to hold them and to bless them (Mark 10:13–16). Jesus welcomed the little children, but he also held them up as an example of

open acceptance of God's kingdom. Young children have the characteristics of trust and openness that we need to emulate in order to receive the kingdom of God ourselves. In other words, Jesus told us to learn from young children!

Children and worship

In Old Testament times it is clear that the Israelites worshipped God as a complete community, including the young children. God gave detailed instructions about how to celebrate the festivals (eg Exodus 12:25–27; Leviticus 23:34 ff) and specified that 'the whole household' was to participate. The household included adult family members, servants, slaves and all the children. Indeed the baby boys were brought into the community of God's people at eight days old, when they were circumcised and shortly afterwards presented and the firstborn redeemed at the Temple. They were included from the earliest stage of life. Even Jesus went through this ceremonial acceptance (Luke 2:21–40).

Samuel gives us one of the few specific examples of God's relationship with young children (1 Samuel 3:1–10). We don't know how old Samuel was when God spoke to him, but he would have been very young when Hannah took him to Eli to begin serving God. God chose to speak to a child about some difficult things. Poor Samuel had to tell Eli that his sons had brought a terrible punishment on their family! Eli did not dismiss Samuel's words, but treated them seriously, as we should do when our children speak about God. Jesus wanted the children to approach him as a man (Matthew 19:14) and Samuel's story indicates that this was not just Jesus' humanity speaking, but that God in his divinity wanted children to hear his voice.

In Jerusalem children joined in the excitement on Palm Sunday, shouting in the Temple. The priests were very upset and appealed to Jesus to restore order (Matthew 21:14–16). (Just imagine your congregation's reaction if the children began shouting in excitement in church!) But Jesus refused, quoting Psalm 8, 'From the lips of children and infants you have ordained praise.' (v 2) The psalm makes clear that young children's praise is welcomed and appreciated and is powerful.

Think about...

Spend some time watching young children as they worship, play and learn. How do they respond to different stimuli? How do they show their love and thanks to their friends and family? Is this how you expect them to show their love and thanks to God?

Jesus reminded the priests of this. This praise from the children was heartfelt and exuberant and definitely not calm and orderly.

PART TWO – IN THEORY: BASIC PRINCIPLES

2

What is worship?

Worship can be defined as 'great or excessive love, admiration, and respect felt for somebody or something' and as the rites or services through which people show this (*Encarta Dictionary*). So for Christians, worship can be seen as any way that our devotion to God can be shown, or those activities that take place during a service that show this. For our purposes we will use the latter of those understandings, including the idea that reading the Bible and hearing teaching about it indicates showing love by wanting to immerse ourselves in God's Word and increase our understanding of him.

More than singing

When we think about worship, most of us immediately think of singing. But a worship service for adults includes music, prayer, hearing from the Bible and other elements. The same applies to under-5s. For under-5s worship can include activities such as singing, music, movement, stories, art and craft and rhymes. We need to include a range of activities for children that together build into a worship experience that teaches and enables the children to develop their relationship with God.

Short but sweet

Young children cannot concentrate for very long, so activities need to be kept short with plenty of variety. As a rule of thumb, it is thought that young children can concentrate for about one minute per year of age. So a 2-year-old concentrates for two minutes and a 4-year-old for approximately four minutes. Of course, sometimes an activity that catches their attention can lead to a much longer focus. The whole worship time needs to be kept short. Depending on the age of the children, how used they are to worship and what else has been happening in their day, a worship time could be as short as ten minutes, and should be at most thirty minutes.

Active
Young children are very active and cannot sit still for very long. So we need to include plenty of activities where the children are moving and doing things, for example, drama, action songs, craft, etc. But be careful to not whip the children up into a state of hyperactivity! When planning your session alternate quiet, reflective activities with more noisy, active ones.

In reality...
Emma's toddler service always begins with the same action song ('If I go climbing' by Julia Plaut). All the children can join in with the actions, pretending to be swimming, driving or climbing. The final verse asks them to pretend they are asleep. The active song ends with the children quietly curled up on the floor. Emma can then easily get the children's attention to listen to the Bible story.

Using repetition
Although young children have short attention spans, they love repetition. Repeating rhymes and songs helps children to learn them and understand them, and helps them extend their attention span. Sometimes the adults get bored first! Having a pattern or a routine to your worship time gives the children a sense of security and order.

Knowing that a certain song will be sung at the beginning or end, or that the story will always be followed by a prayer enables the child to anticipate; learning about the forms of worship and to prepare themselves for the next stage of being with God.

Imitation

Adults are very important to young children. Children look to the adults around them to learn attitudes, to receive guidance and to provide love and security. Because they view adults as important they often copy adults' words and actions. This is a double-edged sword. We need to be careful about what we say and how we act so that the children do not learn bad habits or poor teaching from us. If we get it right, we can teach young children, through our words and actions, by being good role models. We can inspire them to love the Bible, model ways to pray, encourage them to imitate and learn caring ways to treat others and mentor them in their relationship with God. If all the adults present join in, then the children will see that everyone values worship. It is also a very non-threatening way to involve non-Christian parents and carers for whom this may be their only contact with a worshipping group!

Think about...
Reflect on the worship service in your church. In what order do things happen? How do you know what will happen next? What does it feel like when the pattern is changed – exciting or unsettling? Then consider how you can use your thoughts when planning your under-5s worship. Make sure you help the children know what is coming next. Consider where routine is helpful, but don't forget that change can be stimulating in a secure environment.

Developing fast

Babies and 4-year-olds are very different! This is a time of very fast development. During a worship time you will need to be aware of the

Think about...

Spend a little while watching children of different ages. Consider how much a child will have learnt by the age of five. Compare children of different ages – a baby, a toddler and a child about to start school. How have they changed physically and what skills have they learnt?

needs of babies in arms, stumbling toddlers and enthusiastic pre-schoolers.

Understanding

During this time children have limited understanding, but they love to learn. Select the most important points that you want them to learn and explain them in simple ways. In the same way, explain words that may be new to them or, alternatively, substitute other words that communicate the meaning better to them. For example, explain that the Temple was like a very big, special church, or substitute the word 'king' for 'pharaoh'. Not only is a child's vocabulary limited, but their understanding of grammar is also limited, so keep sentences simple and not too long. (Avoid 'could', 'should' and other difficult sentence structures.)

Another area to be aware of is that children's understanding is very literal. If you use abstract concepts, they may find them confusing or even frightening. But chosen carefully and used with appropriate explanation, some 'word pictures' can help young children make connections to their lives outside of the church.

Teaching

In most adult worship services the main teaching is done as a sermon. But children find this harder than adults. Adult sermons frequently have three main points – too much for some adults and certainly too much for small children! Usually, it is best to avoid having a little talk where you explain the teaching point. Instead bring out your simple one-point teaching through your telling of the Bible story and through your choice of songs, rhymes and prayer, etc. Make the theme and connection clear with a short sentence linking the different elements together. Don't belabour your point, but let God speak through the worship.

> **In reality…**
> After a session about God being all around us, as the air and wind are, 4-year-old Anna visited London with her parents. In the underground, as trains moved, Anna felt the rush of wind and exclaimed, 'Mummy, God is here in London too.'

3

PART THREE – PRACTICAL POINTERS

Your venue

When setting up a worship time or service for under-5s you need to consider where it will be taking place. You may have no choice – on a Sunday morning you probably have a certain room. Midweek you may have the choice of the church, a hall or a small room. The key is choosing the most appropriate space (if you can) for the activity types and making the most of it.

It may be tempting to use the church hall, if your under-5s are used to this at toddler group, but you may prefer to use the church as a way of setting the atmosphere and indicating that this is something different and special. Whichever space you use, you will need to make sure that it is welcoming, well lit, appropriately ventilated and heated, clean and safe. It is worth sitting on the floor of your space and looking to see what catches your eye at a child's level. Is the floor clean? Are there electrical sockets or other potential hazards to tempt small fingers? Can you move around freely?

Once you have moved any unnecessary furniture or equipment, you can set up for your under-5s worship. Make sure you have a large space to gather everyone together, where the children can hear and see

the storyteller and have enough space to move. Avoid using chairs for the children, as this restricts their movement, but have some available for the adults who prefer or need them. Think about what the children will see when they are sitting down. This will affect how you present the story especially. If you have a small group, gathering the children around you works well with your storytelling equipment on the floor or a low table. If you have a big group, you will need to raise the level of your equipment so that the children at the back of the group can see and be involved.

Decorating your venue can help to create a welcoming and worshipful atmosphere, especially if you are in an old building. Bunting or streamers can brighten a room very quickly. Balloons look great but are very distracting, and some young children are frightened of them. If you are leading under-5s worship regularly, it is a good idea to have a series of bright banners, which you can hang up quickly to create the right atmosphere without lots of work every week. You could make these with the children and they will love seeing their work used to worship God visually.

In reality...
For under-5s worship in my long, thin, centuries-old church, we clear the chancel putting away communion rails, chairs, music stands and microphones, covering drum kit and electric piano to create our space, with some toys and a craft table at the front of the space with the back left clear for the other aspects of worship. We decorate the length of the church with coloured bunting and leave a trail of stars or footprints, etc to lead the children from the door to the worship space. In the worship space, we sit the children in a semicircle with their parents. Each child has a coloured mat to sit on which helps them to stay still.

Beginning and ending

It is important to start well and end well. How you do both will depend very much on the timing of your worship service, the age of the children, how well you know the families and what has gone on before. The important thing to remember is to make everyone feel welcome and comfortable at the beginning and for them to leave feeling that they have had a good time and wanting to come back for more.

It is very common for under-5s and their carers to arrive over a somewhat protracted period of time. To allow for this, start the session with  an unstructured time, which allows for people to arrive, settle and have something to do. You may choose to serve refreshments, have free play (perhaps linked to your theme) and have a craft to do. Make sure that everyone has a little time to settle before you call everyone to the worship time. You may have a particular song to sing which calls the children to worship. If you have toys out, try to avoid placing these near your worship area or be prepared to put them away when you start your organised worship time.

Think about...

Don't forget that in case of emergency you need to have a sign-in sheet for you, your helpers, the parents and carers and the children. If you intend to take photographs or video, then you need to check that the adults are happy for you to do this.

It is good to finish a session on a positive note with a clear ending. You may choose to close with a prayer or a particular song or by playing an active game together, perhaps with a parachute. Afterwards the families may leave immediately, or you may like to serve refreshments and allow time for free play and craft, which allows the later arrivals to do this as well.

Music

Music is great for creating an atmosphere. If you play quiet music for children to listen to, you teach them that we can be still, and this can give God space to speak. This sort of activity may be difficult for young children at first, but start with just a few seconds the first time and gradually lengthen the time. It can also be a good accompaniment for other activities. Gentle music (with or without lyrics) can create a suitable atmosphere for responsive activities such as drawing or painting. When choosing music for listening to, choose a piece with a simple melody and arrangement. If it is too complex it will not attract the children's attention. The piece you choose needs to sound complete as a very short piece, but you can use the volume control to fade music out. (Have a look at the Baby Einstein range of music; visit www.babyeinstein.co.uk. The short musical tracks are specifically arranged for young children and include classical and traditional favourites.)

Young children love making music using percussion instruments. Make sure you have a good range, with enough for one per child. Allow the children time to play with the instruments so that they can explore the range of sounds they can make and learn to control the instruments. Teach the children a simple visual 'stop' signal in order to regain their attention. The instruments can be used to accompany a song, for sound effects or to express feelings.

In reality…

Rachel asked the children to show her happy sounds with their instruments. Then she asked for sad sounds. As she said the prayer the children played their instruments to reflect the feelings. 'Dear God, we are sorry for all the wrong things we do. We are sorry for hurting people. (*The children played their sad sounds.*) Thank you for all the wonderful things you have given us: families, friends, the warm sunshine and beautiful plants.' (*The children played their happy sounds.*)

Singing

Is it appropriate?

Young children love to sing and we can harness this enjoyment as part of worship. We need to choose songs that are appropriate to the children and fit the overall theme of the worship time. Adults and children develop much of their understanding about God and Jesus through the songs they sing, so it is important that the songs we choose are true to the Bible and focus on God. The words and concepts they use need to be suitable for the children's level of understanding and should make good use of repetition, while being fairly short. Good songs for young children have simple melodies and rhythm (a child's singing range is quite narrow) and are not too fast (or the children will be lost), whilst avoiding dragging.

There are lots of good children's worship songs, and also lots of fun Christian songs which are not worship songs. Ask yourself the question: 'Is this worship?' Worship needs to be God focused. As you read the words, ask these questions:

- Does it show God how much we love him?
- Does it talk to God?
- Does it state truths about God?
- Does it praise the attributes of his character?
- Does it act as a response to God or the Bible?

If you can answer 'yes' to any of these questions, then it is appropriate to use this song for worship. If you can't, then a worship time is not the place for this song. There are other times to use it.

Selecting songs

In any one session try to have a mix of familiar and new songs, so that the children can warm up and feel confident. Where possible, only introduce one new song at a time. Worship is not just about loud excited praise; it is also about feeling God's presence and being quiet before him. Help children to learn this by having a mix of active and more reflective songs. Children love repetition so select a small number of songs and use them several times (in an individual session and over a series of sessions) allowing the children time to learn the songs and be able to move beyond trying to remember them, in order to think about the meaning and focus on God. Wherever possible, link your songs to the theme so that the children continue learning as you worship. You may find that when you have a selection of familiar songs, letting the children choose from them gives them a sense of control over their worship.

Think about...

Look at all the songs your church uses with under-5s. Which ones are good for worship times?

Accompaniment

You don't have to be musical or a good singer to lead children in sung worship. (I'm not!) It is often easiest to sing unaccompanied with young children. Be enthusiastic and confident and the children will join in, without noticing how well you sing. Enlist the parents and carers to add volume and confidence. Give it a go!

If you are fortunate, you may have a good musician to lead worship. You will find that someone else will need to lead the actions and possibly the singing as well. Your musician needs to be aware of the needs of young children, playing at the right speed and volume and using appropriate songs, as described above. If your musician is good and aware of the children's needs, then you can have a brilliant time. If they are not good musically or are unaware of the children's needs, then it can be a disaster! You're better off saying, 'Thank you, but no thank you.'

CDs and music downloads have made life much easier for the non-specialist worship leader. They add much needed 'oomph' to the

In reality...
We often sing 'My very best friend' (Cindy Rethmeier). In the musical fill we shake each others' hands saying, 'Jesus is your friend.' The children love trying to shake everyone's hand.

singing, which can be important in an echoing church building, providing a strong and tuneful lead. Once again, you need to be selective when choosing songs, as some are watered down songs for older children with inappropriate words and uninspiring arrangements. Others are too simplified and 'twee'. Try to listen before you buy. Once you have your songs, be creative in their use. You will often find musical fills occur; think about how you will use these. You could sing the words again, or just do the actions, or you could repeat

Think about...
If you are leading worship, you need to know the words and actions to the songs. Other adults can have them on a screen or paper but the leader needs to be confident. If you are using CDs or mp3 then set up a playlist beforehand so that you have a quick flow between songs.

your teaching point. If the song seems to go on too long, turn it off early, perhaps by fading it out before the last repeat.

Movement

Posture
How we sit or stand makes a huge difference to how we respond to what is happening around us. Standing is ideal for singing as it allows movement for actions and encourages liveliness, but children are more likely to be distracted. Sitting encourages concentration and greater focus so is ideal for quieter, more reflective activities, with fewer opportunities for distraction – lying down even more so.

Actions
Many songs for young children include actions and help children to feel involved quickly. Children who do not know the words of a song or rhyme, who cannot speak or are shy can join in by copying the actions immediately. If you have children with additional needs, using Makaton signs will help them to participate. (Find out more about Makaton at www.makaton.org.)

In reality…
For the first few sessions Lucy didn't want to join in. She would sit still while everyone sang and danced around her. But her mum told us how she sang the songs on the way home. Then one day we waved flags with one song and Lucy joined in enthusiastically with the singing. And she kept singing that day, and the next… It had taken her a while to overcome her reticence, but time, patience and finally the flag had allowed her to become comfortable to join in.

Actions and signs can be very expressive when chosen carefully, and may help understanding when used to illustrate more difficult concepts. The fact that you use actions provides a visual stimulus for the children as well as an aural one. And when the children join in, they have the physical stimulus to help them concentrate. Often we use actions for songs, but we can also use them for prayers, allowing non-verbal children who cannot write or draw to join in and express their emotions.

Think about...

When teaching a new action song, teach the words and actions separately. Encourage the children to join in with the actions as you say the words and then use the actions as you sing the song. Don't try to use too many actions. Choose the key ones for each phrase and the ones that will be repeated during the song.

Dance and drama

Young children have a limited vocabulary and are learning to understand their emotions. Using dance and drama allows them to express their feelings without the need to find words. Both of these involve the whole body and engage the imagination, so help children to focus and join in at their level. Putting on music that reflects the mood of the Bible story and asking the children to move and dance to it helps them, but you may find that you need to be prepared to join in yourself to give them enough confidence to begin. Streamers and small flags add to the range of movement possible and are great fun, often freeing a shy child into excited dance. But don't forget to allow the children time to play with the flags and streamers before you use them for worship.

Involving the children in drama for telling the story helps them get into the story very fully and increases their understanding and memory. For most stories, you will find that everyone acting out the same part at the same time works well, with adults taking additional parts. With a small group, you can easily include dressing up and lots of moving around your worship space. If your group is large, you will need to choose actions that the children can do in a limited space near where they are sitting.

In reality…
One Sunday morning William's mum came up to me. 'All week,' she said, 'we have played with the bricks, building Jericho. Then we march round it, count to seven and then shake the rug to knock the walls down. Then we do it all again.' She was delighted that her 3-year-old had remembered the story of Joshua with such enthusiasm!

Prayer

Communication

Prayer is simply communicating with God. Any way that children use to communicate can be used for prayer. Don't be afraid that children won't say anything. With space, encouragement and experience, children can be amazing in their prayers. They get straight to the point and expect God to answer!

Encourage children to pray, using various forms. Try different methods in order for all the children to find a way that suits them and to keep prayer fresh. However, use one style for a few weeks so the children grow in confidence as you model prayer and give them space to try it for themselves. Using music will enable songs to be used as prayers or as a background to set the mood; instruments can be used to express feelings. Most prayers in church are spoken and, with confidence, young children can pray freely. Start them off with one-word prayers, such as, 'Thank you God for…' Children love to use different volumes, so whispering and shouting prayers will get them engaged. Try choosing a simple phrase to be repeated; start in a whisper and gradually increase the volume, until it is shouted out. Don't forget that the children can pray silently for a very short time. This allows them some privacy in their relationship with God and encourages them to listen to God. (An important part of communicating is listening to the other person!) Quiet music can help this seem less oppressive and mask outside noises.

The upper end of the age range will be able to draw their prayers, which can be kept private or displayed as a group prayer. It does not matter if the adults cannot recognise the drawings. The children are not communicating with them, but with God and he is big enough to know what they have drawn!

Many adults remember learning prayers as a child. (Can you complete this? 'Thank you for the world so sweet…') There is value in doing this, as it models prayer. You could also teach the children a phrase which can be used as a response, while an adult leads the prayers. Try to keep these short and use simple words that the children understand. Generally, I wouldn't recommend the Lord's Prayer for this age group, as it is relatively long and the words, even in the modern version, are difficult for young children.

If you have an active group, you may have difficulty getting them to sit still; harness their energy by using dance or actions to pray or have simple prayer stations around the room.

'How do I get their attention to pray?'

This is a frequent cry from many people with a group of lively young children. There are plenty of ways to do this. For example, going straight from another activity, such as singing or a story, can make this much easier. The old classic of 'hands together, eyes closed' has its place. It reduces distractions and can create a good atmosphere. You could also try holding hands in a circle, or praying with hands outstretched or raised. A prayer drill involves a short series of actions that get the children's attention and can focus them. For example, 'Shake out the fidgets. (*shake hands and legs*) Reach up to get God's attention (*reach up like a child grabbing a parent's hand*), and bring his hand down to your heart (*bring hand down clenched to chest*).' Using a picture or an object as a focus of attention, especially if it is linked to your theme, can also provide a stimulus for prayer.

Think about...

Having a routine helps young children to focus, so decide what best gains their attention and calms them: movement, your voice, music, etc. Now, how can you harness these to signal that now is a time to talk to God? Try out a few ideas on your own and find something that you think will work that you are comfortable doing. Try it with the children. If it works, use this regularly as part of your worship routine to indicate that now it is time to pray.

Not just a wish list

Knowing what to pray about can be worrying for leaders. Using age-appropriate prayer books allows for prayer to be modelled to children and may be a good place to start. They could learn the short ones and then begin adapting them to be more personal. Using the TSP format (**t**hank you, **s**orry, **p**lease) is good on occasions, but needs to allow space for the children to be involved. Pictures and objects related to your theme can help prompt the children. You could put pictures between the pages of the Bible for the children to open up and then pray about, or put them into a bag and draw out one at a time, or place them around the room for children to go to and pray independently. It is important that we teach the children that prayer is not a 'wish list' to God. Encourage the children to listen to God and expect him to communicate with them. Use music, pictures or your voice to create the atmosphere for short quiet times when the children can be aware of God talking to them.

Bible story

Bible time
Basing your worship around a Bible story keeps it grounded on God rather than just having a fun time together. Before you plan your worship, read the story you are using in your Bible so that you remind yourself what it is really about. Then choose which aspect of the story

you feel is most important – your teaching point. If you are planning to tell the story yourself then read your Bible again, pray and write it out. Read it through to make sure that it is clear and then practise telling it. If you are reading from a children's Bible, check that it is accurate to the Bible and draws out your teaching point. If it doesn't, then adapt it as necessary, making notes for yourself as to what you need to add, explain or miss out.

Words
Remember that young children are still learning language and words need to be kept simple or explained. Sentences need to be short and uncomplicated so that the youngest children can follow them. As young children have short concentration spans the whole story needs to be brief – three or four minutes at most. If you are telling a long story, such as Christmas, Easter or Joseph, break it into smaller sections interspersed with other activities.

Involvement
Getting the children involved in the story makes the story come alive for them. Use action and their senses to engage them. Involve the children in copying actions, acting out the story and dressing up to add to the experience.
Sight – use pictures or props or small-world figures.
Sound – add simple sound effects as you tell the story which the children can join in with if they are repeated, or use instruments to create specific sounds or moods.
Taste – if your story involves food then give the children some of it, eg bread, fish paste sandwiches, frosted flakes for manna etc or party food for a celebration story. (But be aware of any potential allergies in your group.)

Smell – this is easier with a small group, but you can use flowers, fresh bread, perfume, etc.

Touch – combined with other senses this can be very powerful, so have sand or water where it fits with the story, stones to hold or a baby doll wrapped in a blanket to cuddle.

In reality...
With small groups I use small plastic figures and coloured fabric to tell the story. The children listen intently. Afterwards they love to use the figures to retell the story themselves.

Rhymes

Rhymes can be sung or spoken and usually have actions that emphasise the words. They can be used to repeat the story or to engage with the teaching theme in a fun way. If printed on a sheet to take home (perhaps alongside a picture) they can be used at home as well.

Art and craft

Art and craft activities can be used in various ways in worship. Prayers can be drawn and open-ended art activities can be used for the children to make their own responses to a story, music or song. Linking a craft to the theme or the story may provide a takeaway item that acts as a reminder at home. If you are looking for an activity to occupy children before the worship starts or after it ends, art and craft activities are good for a productive time filler.

Play

Play activities used at the beginning or conclusion of the worship time can be linked to the theme or story, so that the children connect the worship with the rest of their lives. If you have a large enough space, playing some games together, especially if you have a parachute, enhances the sense of community that is part of worship and can be an exciting way to finish your worship.

TEN TOP TIPS

- Talk to parents and carers to find out what they would like to help their children worship God.
- When choosing a day and time for your worship, find out what else is going on in the lives of the children and select the best time.
- Talk to others (adults and children) about what helps them to worship.
- Take time to prepare fully so that you are ready.
- Keep your theme to one learning point, which you draw out through all the different parts of your worship.
- Remember that less is more. If you try to cram too much in, you will create a stressful atmosphere. Leave space to repeat enjoyable activities, for some to overrun and for God to work.
- Remember that this worship is about the children and God – their relationship is the most important at this time.
- Respect what the children have to bring to the worship, whether it is a stone from the car park or a testimony of God at work in their lives, or their open trust.
- Be prepared to be surprised! Children will surprise you with their insights and God will make his presence known in powerful ways.
- Spend time with God worshipping him and praying to him, so that you are tuned in to him before you plan and prepare to lead children's worship.

RESOURCES

Websites

Tiddlywinks training features in the 'Questions and answers' section of www.scriptureunion.org.uk/tiddlywinks:
- 'Music and worship'
- 'Praying' (2 articles)

Bubbles training features http://www.scriptureunion.org.uk/Light/WebResourcesDownloads/TrainingResources/Bubblestraining/43728.id:
- 'Creative prayer with under-5s'
- 'Inspired storytelling'
- 'Musically challenged?'
- 'Worship the under-5s way'

www.engagetoday.org.uk/playtime – playtime resources for toddler group leaders

www.scriptureunion.org.uk/tiddlywinks – downloadable ideas, links to resources, training articles and much more.

Books

Judith Wigley, *Pretty much everything you need to know about working with under 5s*, Scripture Union, 2005

Judith Merrell, *Ultimate Creative Prayer*, Scripture Union, 2008

Maggie Barfield, *My Big Prayer Book*, Scripture Union, 2010

Maggie Barfield, *Tiddlywinks Say and Sing*, Scripture Union, 2006

Alison Harris, *Praise and Play!* BRF, 2009

Kathryn Copsey and Jean Elliott, *Top Tips on Communicating God in Non-Book Ways*, Scripture Union, 2008

Gill Marchant, Sue Brown and Andy Gray, *Top Tips on Sharing Bible Stories*, Scripture Union, 2008

Sarah Bingham and Vicki Blyth, *Top Tips on Prompting Prayer*, Scripture Union, 2008

Terry Clutterham and John Stephenson, *Top Tips on Discovering the Bible with Children*, Scripture Union, 2009

CDs
Julia Plaut, *Mr Cow*, Kingsway, KMCD2919
Pre-school Praise (series) Spring Harvest
Ishmael, *Be Happy & Be Glad*, Kingsway, CHMCD047
Ishmael, *Ish in the Box 2*, Kingsway, KMCD2987